Our Community Cookbook

A collection of recipes from second graders
at University of Hartford Magnet School
and leaders in the greater Hartford community

This book is dedicated to
the family members and friends
whose heritage and traditions
have touched our lives, and will
continue to touch many in
generations to come.

Illustrated by Taylia

Our Community Cookbook

A collection of recipes from second graders
at University of Hartford Magnet School
and leaders in the greater Hartford community

Written by:

2003-2004 Second Grade Students

at University of Hartford Magnet School

and members of the greater Hartford community

Sponsored by:
The History and Heritage through the Arts Team
Third Age Initiative, Leadership Greater Hartford

Manor Books

PUBLISHED BY MANOR BOOKS

Copyright © 2004 by University of Hartford Magnet School
ISBN: 0-9744752-9-7

Front cover illustration by Pedro.

Back cover illustration by Zhanel.

This book was printed in the United States of America.

Contents

Some of Dr. Johnson's class in the Green Room at Bushnell Theater

Some of Mrs. Febo-Mejia's students in the classroom

Acknowledgments

We wish to acknowledge the following people who have worked so diligently with the students on this project to make it all happen and to those without whose help we could not have gone forward.

Joanne Febo-Mejia – Second grade teacher

Dr. Scott Johnson – Second grade teacher

Cheryl Kloczko – Principal, University of Hartford Magnet School

Dr. Walter Harrison – President, University of Hartford

Ted Carroll and Staff – Leadership Greater Hartford

Dr. and Mrs. David Mucci – Parents and Publisher of this Cookbook

Our many contributors – who have contributed both recipes and money

With our sincere thanks,

The History and Heritage through the Arts Team

Third Age Initiative, Leadership Greater Hartford

Ethel M. Austin, Hartford, Connecticut

Ruth Dorfman, West Hartford, Connecticut

William H. Gerber, West Simsbury, Connecticut

Barbara Pigford, East Granby, Connecticut

Ruth Rabinowitz, Farmington, Connecticut

Robert Wilder, Bloomfield, Connecticut

Introduction

We are pleased to offer the University of Hartford Magnet School community this wonderful cookbook. The second graders in our classes are very proud of their work. It is very exciting to see your work in published form, and they learned many lessons preparing it.

This cookbook is one part of the second grade Social Studies curriculum unit, "What is Community? Examining Our Arts, History, and Heritage". The good people of the *Leadership Greater Hartford Third Age Initiative* wanted to make a lasting contribution to the Greater Hartford community, and thought there was no better way than to help influence the lives of the area's young people. Beginning last year with Principal Cheryl Kloczko and the second grade teachers and students, they developed the framework for this curriculum unit.

The essential understandings of the unit are:
- Knowing ourselves, our family, our neighbors, and where we live, helps us make meaning in our lives
- We make meaning in our lives by interacting with people in our family, our neighborhood, and our environment
- People in a community share, cooperate, solve problems, and serve their community together
- The Arts help us understand the community and ourselves.

The recipes, stories, and drawings in this cookbook reflect the history and heritage of the students and their friends in the community. In completing this book, the children explored the backgrounds of their families and community members. They helped design and illustrate the cookbook, thereby using the principles of Dr. Howard Gardner's theory of multiple intelligences.

We are grateful to the parents and other community members who assisted us in preparing not only this book, but also the other projects that supported our "What is Community?" unit. In particular, we extend our thanks to David and Jeanne Mucci, and the members of the *Third Age Initiative*. Their enthusiasm, energy and expertise allowed the students to develop a product that will provide lasting impressions about the true meaning of "Community".

Bon appetite!

Dr. Scott Johnson and Mrs. Joanne Febo-Mejia
Grade 2 Teachers

Good food is...

"Pizza, because it makes my tongue happy."

Demetrius, age 8

"Applesauce, because you can just swallow it. You don't have to chew it."

Jenny, age 7

"Green apples, because they are tasty and sour."

Paige, age 7

What is good food?

By Ethel M. Austin

Age 89

The History and Heritage through the Arts Team

Third Age Initiative, Leadership Greater Hartford

Today very little time is typically spent preparing meals. Many people are used to popping prepared meals in the microwave. This makes it almost impossible to achieve the three requirements for good food: yummy taste, attractive appearance and food with a pleasant texture.

Husbands and wives who have eaten different culinary combinations all their lives find their children, without anything to compare meals with, often protest they "just don't like it."

Good meals can only be achieved if quality ingredients are used. Whether fresh, canned or frozen, the ingredients must be top quality.

Seasoning is most important and salt is necessary to bring out that taste. However, if salt is banned from the diet by a doctor's orders, other spices and mixtures can be used successfully.

When specific brands are used in a recipe received from a friend or family member, make the recipe exactly as given. Substituting margarine for butter can affect texture, taste and also appearance.

Good food takes time and patience...Good luck to you!

Appetizers

Nana Sylvia's Potato Latkes from Caroline
Papa a la Huancaina from Paige

My Nana holding latkes

Illustrated by Caroline

Nana Sylvia's Potato Latkes
from Caroline

This is one of my favorite foods to eat during the Chanukah holiday, the festival of lights. This recipe is from my great grandmother, Nana Sylvia, from Poland.

Ingredients:
2 pounds Russet potatoes
1 medium yellow onion
2 large eggs
½ cup matzo meal
2 teaspoons kosher salt
½ teaspoon cracked black pepper
Vegetable oil for frying

Grate the potatoes and onions in a food processor, using the shredding blade. Remove mixture to a bowl and replace with the steel "s" blade. In batches, pulse-process the mixture for 10-15 seconds. Place mixture in a strainer over a bowl and squeeze out extra liquid.

Place strained potatoes in a medium sized bowl. Stir in eggs, matzo meal, salt and pepper. Mix well.

In a large skillet, preferably cast iron, heat vegetable oil. Oil should be one inch deep. Scoop two heaping spoonfuls of mixture into pan and flatten (a small ice cream scoop works great!). Cook for 6-8 minutes or until gold, flip and cook for an additional 3-4 minutes or until golden as well. Drain pancakes on a paper towel. Serve with sour cream, chives and caviar if desired.

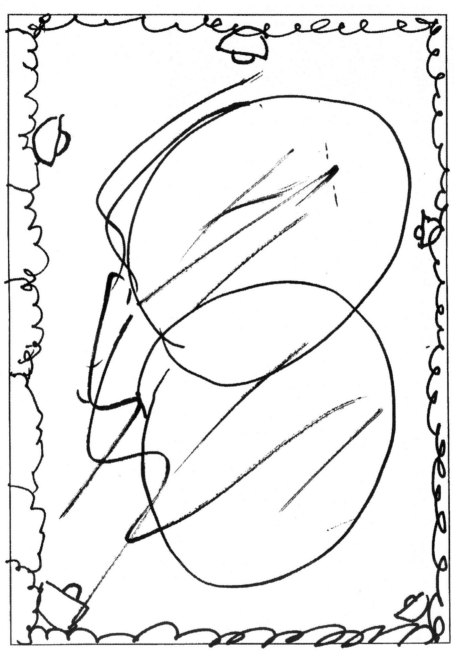

Illustrated by Paige

Papa a la Huancaína
(Boiled Potatoes with Yellow Sauce)
from Paige

This recipe is originally from Peru. My mom's family cooks this recipe on birthdays, holidays and special occasions. This recipe is cooked on almost every special occasion because my mother's grandfather used to have a farm where they grew potatoes and vegetables, so for them it was easy to get all the ingredients.

Ingredients:
2 cups of water
6 potatoes
2 spoonfuls of yellow pepper (from Peru)
6 ounces of cream cheese
20 pieces of crackers
1 can of milk
1 teaspoon of salt
2 boiled eggs
lettuce, black olives, parsley to decorate this dish

Boil the potatoes in the water. After they are cooked, peel and cut each in half.

In blender, blend yellow pepper, cream cheese, crackers, and milk. Add salt and pepper to taste. This sauce is supposed to be creamy enough to pour on top of the potatoes.

Place the lettuce on a dish around the edges, and potatoes in the middle
of the dish. Cover with the "yellow" sauce. Place some black olives on top and a little bit of parsley.

Cut the hard boiled eggs in 4 pieces each and place on top of the potatoes.

Soups & Stews

Beef Stew from Chance

Chicken Soup from Ben M.

Nana's Italian Meatball and Escarole Soup from Dr. Mucci

Beef Stew
from Chance

This is one of my favorite dishes to eat. It is a fairly new recipe—invented by our family. We often serve it with hot bread or homemade corn muffins. It changes every time we make it depending on what we want at that time. We might add different veggies, make the gravy thicker or thinner, make the beef into strips, tiny cubes, try different spices, etc. Changing the recipe makes it fun and never boring!

Ingredients:
3 pounds of beef, cut into cubes
1 cup flour
1 teaspoon each of garlic powder, onion powder, pepper, paprika
½ teaspoon salt
Olive oil for browning
3 cans beef broth (low salt)
1 small onion
3 cloves of garlic, chopped
½ cup white wine
5 pounds of potatoes, peeled and cubed
2 pounds of carrots, peeled and diced
1 jar boiling onions

Pour oil into pan and heat at medium. Pour two cans of broth into a large pot and heat at medium high.

Mix flour and seasonings in a large (one gallon) zip lock bag. Add beef to bag and shake to coat well. Put floured beef into heated oil and cook until mostly browned.

Transfer meat to heated broth and bring to a boil. Meanwhile, sauté onion and garlic, and then add to meat and broth. Once boiling, turn heat to medium low and stir often. If meat begins to stick, turn to low. Cook for 30 minutes.

Add carrots, potatoes and wine. If there is not enough gravy, add more broth—small amounts at a time. Cook until potatoes and carrots are tender. Add onions 10 minutes before serving.

Illustrated by Chance

Chicken Soup
from Ben M.

My Mom cooks chicken soup whenever anyone in our family is sick. She also makes it on Halloween night to warm us up after trick-or-treating. Sometimes she cooks it for dinner just because I like it so much. This recipe has been passed from mother to daughter for generations. My Mom learned to make it from her Mom.

Ingredients:
1 whole chicken 4-6 pounds, rinsed and cleaned well (remove gizzards from inside chicken and toss out)
18 cups of water
1 large clove of garlic, peeled
2 teaspoons of seasoned salt
1 tablespoon of regular table salt
1 whole onion, brown peeling removed
6 stems of parsley, chopped (if you don't like to eat parsley, like our family, tie the parsley into a bundle with string)
1 celery stalk, diced into ½" pieces
1 cup of carrots, peeled and diced into ½" pieces
1 small parsnip, peeled and diced into ½" pieces
1 small purple top turnip, peeled and diced into ½" pieces
Optional 1 teaspoon Emerill's Essence or Cajun Seasoning
8 ounces of tomato sauce

Put the first seven ingredients in a large soup pot. Cover and bring to a boil on high heat. Use a large spoon and skim off any fat and foam on the surface of the soup. Put remaining ingredients in the soup pot. Bring to a boil, and then lower to a simmer. Simmer for one hour. Skim any remaining fat off the surface of the soup. Remove chicken and clean meat off bones. Put some of the chicken back in the soup and discard bones. (Rest of chicken can be saved for another meal or made into chicken salad). Remove and discard whole onion, garlic clove, and bundle of parsley (if you tied up the parsley). Boil one pound of small pasta noodles (ditalani, teardrops, or any shape you'd like). Add noodles to soup bowls before ladling in the soup.

My great grandmother Polacheck would cook chicken soup every Sunday for dinner, and make homemade noodles to go with it. She made soup the old-fashioned, Slovak style. She would stuff the chicken with bread stuffing and sew it up tight, then put the chicken, some potatoes, and a bunch of whole vegetables in the soup pot to cook. She would serve soup as a first course, then serve the chicken, stuffing, and vegetables as the main course. We like to eat the chicken and vegetables cut up in our soup, so Mom makes it a little different today for our family.

Illustrated by Ben M.

Dr Mucci discusses how Emergency Room physicians help members of the community. Second graders experience wearing surgical masks and gloves.

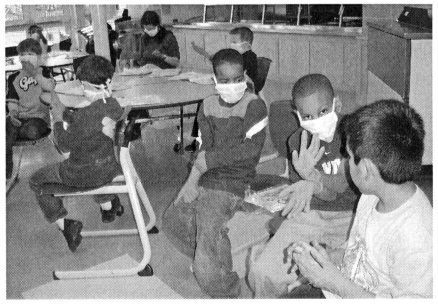

Nana's Italian Meatball and Escarole Soup
From David A. Mucci, M.D., Emergency Room Physician

When I was in elementary school we didn't have a cafeteria to eat lunch in. We walked home for lunch in the middle of the school day. On cold days my mom always had a hot pot of soup ready for us at lunchtime. This soup was my favorite.

Ingredients:
1 gallon chicken broth (16 cups)
1 head of escarole
½ cup water
½ pound of ground beef
½ pound of small pasta (orzo or ditalani work well)
salt, pepper, garlic to taste
1 cup chopped root vegetables (carrots, turnip, parsnip, whatever you like)

Rinse the escarole. Cut off the bottom to remove the core. Put the escarole in a small pot with ½ cup of water. Bring to a boil and then let boil for three minutes. Remove from heat and let cool. Chop up the escarole into small pieces once cool. Cooking the escarole before putting it in the soup remove the bitterness.

Heat three cups of the chicken broth in a small 2-quart pot. Make pea-sized meatballs from the ground beef and put them in the hot chicken broth. Bring the broth to a boil. Once the meatballs are floating they have cooked (just takes a few minutes). Drain the broth out of the meatballs and discard the broth.

In a large soup pot heat the remaining chicken broth. Add the cooked escarole, cooked meatballs, seasonings, root vegetables, and bring to a boil. Once boiling, add the pasta and cook until the pasta is soft (about 15 minutes). Can serve with grated Parmesan cheese sprinkled on top, if desired.

Entrees

Blueberry French Toast from Alexander

Braised Steak with Onions from Taj

Breakfast Eggs from Madeline McKernan, Community Liaison at
University of Hartford Magnet School

Breakfast on a Stick from Acting Chief Michael Parker, Hartford Fire
Department

Cajun Shrimp over White Rice from Shateria

Chicken Breast in Alfredo Sauce from Devin

Crepes from Zachary

Curried Goat from Jazzmin

Meat Rolled in Cabbage from Ruth Dorfman, History and Heritage
through the Arts Team

Meat Sauce for Pasta from Cheryl Kloczko, Principal, University of
Hartford Magnet School

Pesto Pasta from Ernie

Puerto Rican Rice with Chicken (Arroz Con Pollo) from Joanne Febo-
Mejia, second grade teacher at University of Hartford Magnet
School

South of the Border Chicken from Kathy Neuhaus,
Interpersonal/Intrapersonal Skills Teacher at University of
Hartford Magnet School

Stewed Chicken from Zhanel

Veal Marsala from Dakota

Blueberry French Toast

from Alexander

This recipe is from an old family cookbook. Everyone loves it and asks for it _every_ year. Mom makes it Christmas Eve and bakes it Christmas morning. On Christmas morning, my two older brothers and nephews come over to open presents and after, we have brunch

Ingredients:
1 loaf Challah bread, cut into 1" cubes
1 cup fresh or frozen blueberries
2 packages (8 ounces each) cream cheese
12 eggs
2 cups milk
1/3 cup maple syrup

Ingredients for sauce:
1 cup sugar
2 tablespoons cornstarch
1 cup water
1 cup fresh or frozen blueberries
1 tablespoon butter

Place half of cubed bread in greased 13 x 9 glass baking dish. Cut cream cheese into 1" cubes and place over bread. Top with blueberries and remaining bread.

In large bowl beat eggs. Add milk and syrup, mix well. Pour over bread mixture, cover and chill 8 hours or overnight.

Remove from refrigerator 30 minutes before baking. Cover with foil and bake at 350° for 30 minutes. Uncover and continue baking 25-30 minutes until golden brown.

In saucepan combine sugar, cornstarch and water, and bring to boil. Boil three minutes over medium heat, stirring constantly. Stir in blueberries; reduce heat. Simmer for 8-10 minutes or until berries have burst. Stir in butter until melted. Serve sauce over french toast.

Illustrated by Alexander

Braised Steak with Onions
From Taj

My family was first served this recipe, from my Mom's cookbook, at a family cookout. My family does not eat beef much because the meat comes out so tough when it's cooked. So it took some convincing to get my family to try this recipe, even though my Mom very carefully followed the directions. The steak came out really tender. My grandmother performed a fork test to see how tender it was, and ended up almost eating the whole steak.

Ingredients:
4 pounds Sirloin butt, cut into 6 ounce slices
5 ounces oil
Seasoned flour, as needed
12 ounces Mirepoix
4 ounces red bell pepper, cut brunoise (finely chopped)
6 ounces red wine
1 quart demi-glace, heated to boil
2 pounds of onions, peeled and cut julienne
1 tablespoon Hungarian sweet paprika
Salt and freshly ground black pepper
3 ounces fresh parsley, washed, excess moisture removed and chopped

Preheat oven to 350 degrees. Pound meat with a heavy mallet to tenderize. In a braising pan, heat 3 ounces of oil. Dredge steaks in flour, shake off excess and sear on both sides. Remove from pan and reserve.

In the same pan sauté mirepoix and peppers until lightly browned. Deglaze pan with the wine and simmer 2 minutes. Add demi-glace.

Return steaks to the sauce and coat well. Remove steaks to an ovenproof pan and seal pan with aluminum foil. (Reserve sauce for later.) Braise steaks in oven until tender, about 45 minutes. Keep warm at 140-degree oven until ready to serve.

In another sauté pan, heat remaining oil and sauté onions until they become translucent. Add paprika and sauté one minute more, or until oil turns red. Season to taste and hold at 140 degrees.

Strain sauce through a chinois mousseline. Adjust consistency and seasonings of sauce to taste. Also hold at 140 degrees until ready to serve. Garnish with parsley before serving.

Helping out each other

Illustrated by Taj

Madeline McKernan with two second graders.

Make ahead Breakfast Eggs

from Madeline McKernan, Community Liaison at
University of Hartford Magnet School

Ingredients:
1 dozen eggs
½ cup milk
½ teaspoon salt
½ teaspoon pepper
1 tablespoon butter
1 8-ounce container sour cream
12 slices of bacon, cooked and crumbled
1 cup shredded sharp cheddar cheese

In a medium bowl beat eggs, then stir in milk, salt, and pepper. Set aside.

In large skillet, over medium low heat, melt butter. Pour in egg mixture. Cook, stirring occasionally until eggs are set but still moist. Remove from heat to cool.

Stir sour cream into the cooked egg mixture. Spread evenly into a buttered two-quart shallow baking dish. Top with bacon and cheese.

Cover with aluminum foil and refrigerate overnight. Preheat oven to 300 degrees. Uncover eggs. Bake 15-20 minutes or until hot and cheese had melted.

Acting Fire Chief, Michael Parker, from the Hartford Fire Department spoke to the second graders about how the fire department helps keep the community safe. He reminded the children what a smoke detector sounds like and what to do in the event of a fire. He warned the students about the dangers of playing with fire, and informed everyone that many house fires start from allowing decorative candles in jars to burn to the bottom of the jar.

Breakfast on a stick

from Acting Chief M. A. Parker, Hartford Fire Department

Ingredients:
12 ounces hot or sweet sausage
8 hard-boiled eggs
4 eggs
½ cup all-purpose flour
½ cup corn flour
2 teaspoons crushed dried sage
2 teaspoons crushed dried thyme
Pinch of cayenne pepper
1 cup seasoned breadcrumbs

Preheat oven to 450 degrees.

Wrap each hard cooked egg with sausage, ensuring the entire egg is completely covered.

Combine the corn flour and all-purpose flour in a bowl.
In a separate bowl, beat the 4 eggs with a tablespoon of water.
In a third bowl mix together the seasoned bread crumbs, sage, thyme, and cayenne pepper.

Roll each sausage-covered egg in the flour, shaking off the excess, dip in the egg, then the seasoned breadcrumbs.

If baking – place a 4-inch stick (candy apple stick) in each prepared egg and spray with cooking oil (Pam). Place in a baking dish and bake in the 450-degree oven for 15-20 minutes or until nicely browned and crisp. Cool and enjoy.

If deep-frying – place eggs in the basket and slowly place in the deep fryer. Cook for 8-10 minutes. Cool, then place the stick in the egg and enjoy.

Illustrated by Shateria

Cajun Shrimp over White Rice

from Shateria

I love to eat these Cajun shrimp. It's spicy, so I make sure I have juice to drink when I eat it.

I love to eat these Cajun shrimp. It's spicy, so I make sure I have juice to drink when I eat it.
2½ pounds frozen shrimp
2 tablespoons butter
2 tablespoons Cajun seasoning (or amount to taste)
2 dashes of salt
2 dashes of pepper
2 cups white rice
1 teaspoon vegetable oil

Place shrimp in a bowl and rinse. Season them with Cajun seasoning, salt and pepper. Melt butter in pan and add shrimp. Cover and simmer 5-7 minutes. While the shrimp is simmering, boil water for rice. Once water comes to a boil add vegetable oil and salt to taste, and rice. Cook covered for 20 minutes. Spoon shrimp over cooked rice. Serve.

Illustrated by Devin

Chicken Breasts in Alfredo Sauce
from Devin

My family likes to eat this chicken dish for dinner. It's one of my favorites.

Ingredients:
2 jars of Classico Alfredo sauce
1 bag (one pound) of egg noodles
3 skinless chicken breasts or 1 package of chicken breast tenderloins (skinless)
salt
pepper
garlic powder
½ tablespoon margarine
¼ cup of vegetable oil

Put vegetable oil into water with egg noodles and bring to a boil, making sure noodles are soft. While noodles are cooking, you can season chicken breasts with the garlic powder and pepper. Put the ½ tablespoon of margarine into the frying pan, add chicken breast strips, and cook 3 – 5 minutes on each side.

When the noodles are done, strain the water off of them. Set them to the side.

Pour the two jars of Alfredo sauce into a pot. Let simmer and stand. While Alfredo sauce is simmering, cut some chicken breasts into little squares and put them into the sauce. Next add noodles and stir. Add more cut up chicken and noodles and stir. Continue adding all the chicken and noodles. Mix it all well, and then you have dinner in 15 minutes.

Dad making Crepes

Illustrated by Zach

Crepes
from Zachary

This recipe was passed down from my dad's Grandmother to my dad's Mom. Now my Dad often makes them for us on Fridays during Lent. These crepes are so good that I don't ever miss eating meat on Fridays.

Ingredients:
1 cup flour
1 cup milk
2 eggs
1 cup water

Stir all the ingredients together, so there are no lumps. Cook in a hot skillet. Makes four crepes. Sprinkle with brown sugar after cooking.

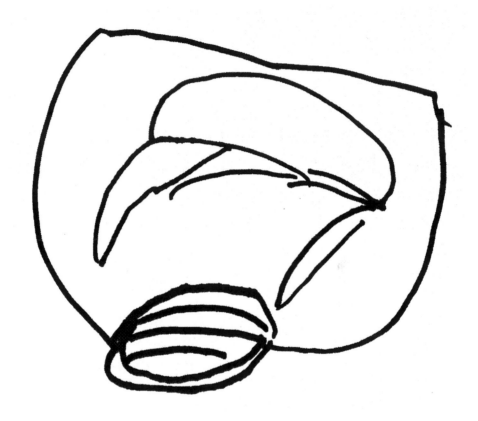

Illustrated by Jazzmin

Curried Goat

from Jazzmin

This recipe is a common dish in Jamaica. Curried goat is an important part of the meal during Sunday dinners. Curried goat is also prepared at other family gatherings such as Reunions and Funerals. Years ago when the family got together, they would get one of their goats, and kill it for the mutton and use other parts of the goat to make soup.

Ingredients:
2 pounds mutton
2 tablespoons cooking fat
1 tablespoon curry powder
½ pound diced potato
2 cups water
1 teaspoon salt
1 large onion
2 peppers
1 teaspoon black pepper

Clean and cut meat into one-inch cubes. Season properly with salt, pepper and onions. Rub in curry and allow to stand for about ½ hour.

Heat fat in frying pan and fry briskly. Add water, cover tightly and allow to cook slowly until meat is tender. Put in potatoes and cook until gravy becomes somewhat thick.

This can be served either with rice or green bananas, or both.

Illustrated by Ajia

Good Food is...

"hotdogs, because I like ketchup and mustard."

— Kory, age 7

"pizza, because the pepperoni is spicy."

— Alexander, age 7

"soup, because it makes me happy."

— Shateria, age 8

" sweet and sour."

— Ben A., age 8

"oranges because they are healthy. I like fruit because it is good for you."

— Caroline, age 7

Meat Rolled in Cabbage
from Ruth Dorfman, History and Heritage through the Arts Team

Every Friday night, when I was growing up, our family went to my grandparents' house for Sabbath dinner. The house smelled of freshly made bread. My grandmother would say prayers over the lighted candles and then we'd assemble around the specially set dining room table for a dinner, which often included "meat rolled in cabbage".

Ingredients:
1 head of cabbage
1½ pounds . lean ground meat
1 cup bread crumbs
1 egg
½ can tomato paste
1 small onion, chopped finely
1 large can whole tomatoes
½ can tomato paste
juice of 1 large lemon
4 tablespoons brown sugar
salt and pepper
8 ginger snaps

Cut out core of cabbage. Steam cabbage head in a large pot of boiling water until leaves are softened and loosened. Allow to cool.

Combine next five ingredients well. Put a small ball of meat mixture in each leaf of cabbage and roll up. Place rolls in pot. Combine last six ingredients. Pour over the cabbage rolls. Simmer about 1 ½ hours. Serve with sour cream.

Because it was forbidden to work or light the stove once the Sabbath began, my grandmother would cook and bake all day in preparation. The main course was one that always benefited from long cooking. Every time I make this dish for my family, I think of my grandmother praying over the candles, for all of us, a black lace mantilla on her head.

Good Food is...

"pizza, because it has sauce. I love sauce."
— Joshua, age 7

"spicy foods, because it's really good and my Mom makes good curry chicken."
— Imani, age 8

"soup, because it makes you feel better when you have a cold."
— Chance, age 8

Mrs. Kloczko with a group of second graders.

Meat Sauce for Pasta

from Cheryl Kloczko, Principal, University of Hartford Magnet School

Ingredients:
¼ cup olive oil
1½ pounds of ground round (93% lean)
5 garlic cloves, finely chopped
3 one pound, 12 ounce cans tomato puree
2 six-ounce cans of tomato paste
1 cup dry red wine
1-cup water
2 tablespoons dried basil
2 bay leaves
½ teaspoon hot red pepper flakes
Salt and freshly ground black pepper to taste

Heat the oil in a large heavy saucepan. Add the meat and cook for 10 minutes, stirring occasionally.

Add the garlic to the pan and brown lightly, then add the onions. Sauté until tender.

Add all the remaining ingredients and bring to boil. Lower the heat and simmer for two hours, stirring occasionally.

Refrigerate in airtight containers or freeze in small amounts.

This recipe is similar to the one my grandmother would use to make her pasta sauce on a daily basis when feeding her family of nine children. She would use salt port to sauté the garlic and onion but in our fat counting consciousness I have substituted olive oil. I use all organic meat, vegetables, puree and paste since all her ingredients came from her back yard garden and nearby meat market, which sold beef raised by the local farmer. My grandmother would serve her sauce on homemade pasta, which she also made daily for her family.

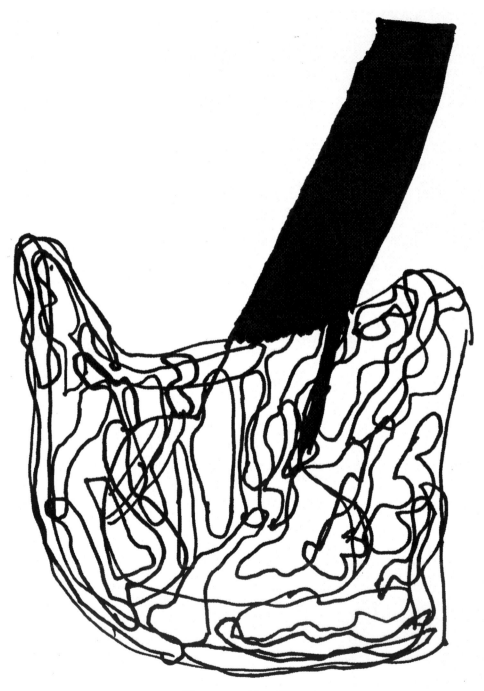

Illustrated by Ernie

Pesto Pasta
from Ernie

This recipe originally came from Italy many generations ago. A family dinner is an event and we enjoy this dinner every week.

Ingredients:
3 cups fresh basil
3 cloves garlic
½ cup olive oil
¼ cup Parmesan cheese
½ teaspoon salt
½ teaspoon pepper
1 pound penne pasta

Add garlic, olive oil, Parmesan cheese, salt, pepper, and half of the basil to a blender. Blend well. Then add remaining basil and blend to form a thick consistency. A little extra oil may be needed.

Boil and cook pasta al dente. Drain pasta and transfer to a bowl. Mix pesto with pasta.
Serve and enjoy.

Every summer my dad grows a bunch of fresh basil in our herb garden. In September I help my dad pick the basil and we make lots of pesto. We put it in containers and freeze it so we can enjoy it all winter.

Puerto Rican Rice with Chicken (Arroz con Pollo)

from Joanne Febo-Mejía, second grade teacher at University of Hartford Magnet School

Arroz con Pollo is one of the main dishes my family has in our gatherings. It was my favorite when I was younger and still is. I used to ask my mother to make this for me and she would. It's funny because I usually don't eat the chicken that's put in the rice, but I love chicken! I've been known to be a picky eater and my family always comments on why I love chicken with rice, if I don't eat the chicken.

In our home while growing up, rice was always served because it was part of our tradition, and because my father needs to have rice EVERY day. Any time I go to my parents' home for dinner, I know that I will eat rice.

Ingredients:
2 peppercorns (whole black-pepper)
2 cloves of garlic, peeled
1 teaspoon dried oregano
4 ½ teaspoons salt
2 teaspoons olive oil
1 tablespoon vinegar

2 ½ pounds chicken pieces

1 tablespoon lard or vegetable oil
1 ounce salt pork, washed and diced
2 ounces lean cured ham, diced

1 onion, peeled and diced
1 green pepper, diced
3 sweet chile peppers, diced
1 tomato, diced
6 fresh cilantro leaves, diced

1 17-ounce can green peas(petitpois)

½ teaspoon salt
10 olives stuffed with pimientos
1 tablespoon capers
¼ cup tomato sauce
2 tablespoons fat or "achiote coloring"
3 cups rice

1 4-ounce can pimientos

Mix and crush together the peppercorns, garlic, oregano, salt, olive oil, and vinegar (the first six ingredients). Wash chicken and divide each chicken piece in two. Dry and rub with the seasoning mixture. Set in refrigerator overnight.

In a "Caldero" or heavy kettle, heat fat and brown rapidly salt pork and ham. Reduce to moderate and add chicken. Cook for 5 minutes. Reduce heat to low. Add the onion, green pepper, sweet chili peppers, tomato, and fresh cilantro leaves. Sauté for 10 minutes stirring occasionally.

Meanwhile drain liquid from can of peas into a measuring cup and enough water to make 2 ½ cups, if regular rice is used or 3 ½ cups if long rice is used. Reserve peas. Heat liquid in a pan and set aside.

Add to kettle the ½ teaspoon salt, olives, capers, tomato sauce, fat or "achiote coloring" and rice. Mix over moderate heat for two minutes. Add hot liquid to kettle and mix well. Cook uncovered over moderate heat until rice is dry. With a fork turn rice from bottom to top. Cover kettle and cook over low heat for 40 minutes. Halfway during this cooking period turn rice over again. Add peas. Turn rice once more and cover, cooking for 15 minutes in low heat.

Spoon rice with chicken onto a serving platter. Heat pimientos in their juices, drain and garnish the rice dish. Serve at once. ENJOY!

Above: Mrs. Febo-Mejia with her class. Below: Second grade
Paraprofessional, Kathy Bell, with two students.

Above: Mayor Perez signs autographs for second graders.
Below: Second grade students listen attentively while Mayor Perez talks to them.

Mrs. Neuhaus teaching second graders to do tableau with a prop, during Interpersonal/Intrapersonal skills class.

South of the Border Chicken

from Kathy Neuhaus, Interpersonal/Intrapersonal skills teacher
at University of Hartford Magnet School

Ingredients:
3-4 pounds boneless chicken meat, cut into small pieces
1 large onion, diced
2 cans cream of chicken soup
2 cans cream of mushroom soup
1 small can green chilies
grated cheddar and Monterey Jack cheese
Corn tortillas

Cook the chicken breast pieces. (Use more meat if you wish).

Sauté the onion. Mix together with the cream of chicken soup, cream of mushroom soup, and green chilies.

Grate cheddar cheese and Monterey Jack cheese. (Amount is determined by how much cheese you like.)

In an 8x12x2 pan, layer the bottom with corn tortillas. Then alternate between soup mixture, cheese mixture, chicken, and tortillas. Top with cheese.

Bake one hour at 325 degrees.

Note: this recipe can be made ahead of time and frozen until you want to serve.

Illustrated by Zhanel

Stewed Chicken
from Zhanel

My mom learned to make this recipe from Grandma Vicky when she was young. It's really good because the chicken is all juicy!

Ingredients:
2 pounds chicken cut in small pieces
2 medium potatoes (chopped)
2 tablespoons oil
4 tablespoons sugar
2 large onions, sliced
1 tablespoon Worcestershire sauce
2 tablespoons soy sauce
2 bay leaves
2 cloves garlic
3 scallions
1 tablespoon basil or thyme
black and hot pepper to taste

Season meat with soy sauce, Worcestershire sauce, and black pepper. Marinate for three hours or overnight.

Heat oil and add sugar. Allow to burn until dark brown and looks like a caramel coating. Add seasoned meat and stir well to coat pieces of meat, for 6-8 minutes.

Add remaining ingredients except potatoes and cook for 20-30 minutes.

Add potatoes and cook until tender.

Illustrated by Dakota

Veal Marsala
from Dakota

My Grandma Jinny makes this recipe for my family to eat on special occasions. I love how tender the meat comes out!

Ingredients:
2 pounds of veal cutlets (unbreaded)
1 pound of fresh cut mushrooms (diced)
1 clove of fresh garlic
1 small onion (chopped fine)
3 sticks of celery (chopped)
¼ cup butter
¼ cup vegetable oil
½ cup flour
½ cup marsala wine
salt and pepper (to taste)
fresh parsley

Sauté chopped onion, celery and garlic in butter and oil in a large skillet. Remove from skillet to small bowl and set aside. Sauté mushrooms quickly and remove to a bowl (brown slightly). Flour veal slices and brown slightly. Remove veal to a plate. Add wine, to skillet and simmer until thickened. Add salt and pepper to sauce in skillet. Strain the sauce to remove lumps, and then add sautéed vegetables to sauce. Place veal and mushrooms in layers in a flat casserole dish that is safe to use on the stovetop. Pour sauce over it and cover. Simmer until ready to serve, and then decorate with fresh parsley.

Side Dishes

Macaroni and Cheese from Ajia

Macaroni and Cheese from Demetrius

Macaroni and Cheese from Gianna

Macaroni and Cheese from Imani

Macaroni and Cheese from Rhyan

Rice Pilaf from Dr. Johnson's Grandmother and Mother, from Dr.
    Johnson, second grade teacher at University of Hartford Magnet
    School

Sausage Stuffing from Kory

Spanish Rice from Officer Rodriguez, Hartford Police Department

Sweet Potato Casserole from Joe

Tsimmes from Ruth Rabinowitz, History and Heritage through the Arts
    Team

Mac and Cheese

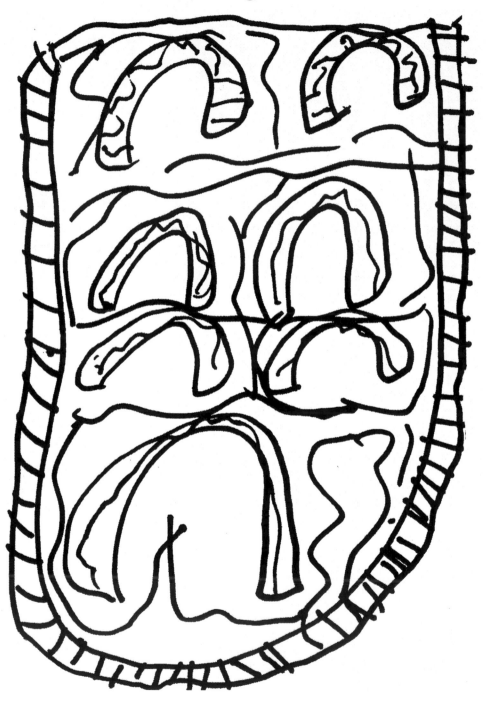

Illustrated by Ajia

Simply Delicious Baked Macaroni and Cheese
from Ajia

The recipe came from my father's mother. Sometimes my grandma comes over and makes it. I love this Macaroni and Cheese recipe.

Ingredients:
2 quarts water
2 teaspoons salt (optional)
2 cups elbow macaroni
2 cups milk
2 large eggs, beaten
2 tablespoons butter, melted
½ teaspoon ground black, white or red pepper
2 cups shredded sharp cheddar cheese
1 teaspoon paprika (optional)

In a large pot, bring water to rapid boil. Stir in salt (if desired) and pasta. Cook, stirring frequently to avoid clumping together and sticking to the pan. Follow cooking directions on package and check for doneness; do not overcook. Pour macaroni in colander to drain. In medium-size bowl stir together milk, eggs, melted butter and pepper. Spoon about 1/3 of macaroni into 2-quart baking dish; top with 1/3 of cheese. Repeat layering, ending with cheese on top. Pour milk mixture over macaroni. Sprinkle lightly with paprika if desired. Bake uncovered until top is crusty and golden brown, about 40 minutes. Makes 8 servings.

My father says he always had this macaroni and cheese at Easter dinner, along with ham as the main course. My father enjoyed watching his mother and grandmother prepare Easter dinner. Their love in the kitchen played big a role in creating the love my father displays when cooking for me, his daughter. He's always wanted to pass on that same fun and happy atmosphere in the kitchen that he enjoyed as a child.

Macaroni and cheese

Illustrated by Demetrius

Macaroni and Cheese
from Demetrius

My grandmother knows I love macaroni and cheese, so she makes this special recipe for me. She brought it this year for Thanksgiving.

Ingredients:
1 pound of macaroni noodles (1 box)
3 tablespoons of butter
1 tablespoon of flour
3 cups of milk
5 cups of shredded cheddar cheese

Boil macaroni for about 20 minutes or until done. Drain macaroni in a strainer.

Melt butter, milk, cheese and flour in a medium pot; stir until cheese is melted smoothly.

Put macaroni in a baking dish and pour melted cheese in with macaroni. Mix melted cheese thoroughly.

Bake in oven at 350 degrees for 45 minutes or until top is crusty brown.

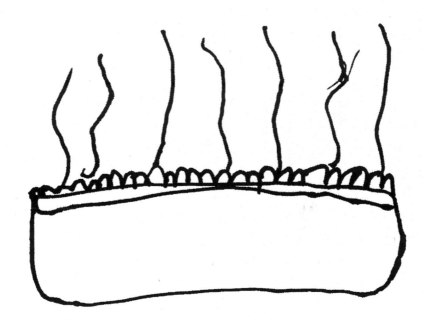

Illustrated by Gianna

Macaroni and Cheese
from Gianna

Let's eat Mississippi homemade macaroni and cheese!

Ingredients:
2 (one pound) boxes elbow macaroni, cooked according to box
       directions
6 eggs
3 pounds shredded cheddar cheese
1 stick margarine, melted
1 pound shredded colby cheese
1 tablespoon seasoned salt
3 tablespoons Morton's salt
½ tablespoon black pepper
2 cups milk
½ teaspoon garlic powder

Mix all ingredients together and put in baking dish. Sprinkle some extra shredded cheese over the top of the mixture. Cover the dish and put in oven at 425 degrees to bake for 1½ hours. Take out and let cool. It's ready.

Cooking Macaroni and Cheese

Illustrated by Imani

Homemade Macaroni and Cheese

from Imani

Ingredients:
1 (one pound) box of elbow macaroni
1 12-ounce package of shredded sharp cheddar cheese
1 12-ounce package of shredded mixed cheeses
1 8-ounce package of Colby cheese (cut into small cubes)
2 cups milk
2 teaspoons of margarine
4 large eggs
1 tablespoon salt
2 tablespoons cream cheese

Boil macaroni until cooked according to package directions. Put into large mixing bowl. Add cheeses. Then add milk, margarine and eggs. Finally, add salt and cream cheese. Mix it all up and pour into a baking pan. Bake about one hour at 400 degrees, or until macaroni is firm. Allow to cool for about ½ hour.

Serving Macaroni and Cheese

Illustrated by Imani

Illustrated by Rhyan

Macaroni and Cheese
from Rhyan

This recipe is from my Mom. We serve it at most family gatherings.

Ingredients:
1½ pounds of elbow macaroni
1 pound extra sharp New York cheddar cheese, grated
4 cups milk
1 large onion, finely chopped (but not minced)
1 stick butter
season with salt to taste
black pepper, optional
bread crumbs for topping
3 – 4 heaping tablespoons all-purpose flour
nonstick spray

Cook and drain macaroni. Heat oven to 400 degrees.

Sauté onion in 1/2 stick of butter (on medium heat). When onions are almost translucent, add remaining butter and flour. Cook onion-butter-flour mixture until a thick, pasty consistency. Add milk. Cook entire mixture until bubbly. Add salt and pepper to taste. Add cheese. Cook on high for a little less than two minutes, then turn down to low. Cook another three minutes, until all cheese is melted.

Add this sauce to macaroni. Stir until entire mixture is consistent, and each macaroni is coated with cheese mixture.

Spray baking dish (13 x 9 pyrex glass dish works well) with nonstick spray. Pour macaroni mixture into baking dish. Top with bread crumbs and nonstick spray (so breadcrumbs won't burn). Bake at 400 degrees for 25 – 40 minutes (depending on your oven) until cheese is bubbling and bread crumbs are golden.

Serves 8 -10. Recipe can be doubled.

Dr. Johnson's Grandmother's and Mother's Rice Pilaf

from Dr. Scott Johnson, second grade teacher
at University of Hartford Magnet School

My parents both grew up in Hartford. My mother's side of the family is Armenian, and my favorite Armenian food is Rice Pilaf. We would have this at almost every meal where chicken, beef, or lamb was served, especially holidays. I can remember my grandmother making this and showing my mother how to make it. When I was growing up, my mother taught *me* how to cook it. And now, I have taught my daughter how to make it, too! Sometimes it is hard to get the rice to come out fluffy. But when it does, it is so delicious!

Ingredients:
1 cup white rice
1 small can (14 oz.) *College Inn* chicken broth
Water
Thin egg noodles (about 1 half cup)
Margarine (about 6 tsp.)
Salt and pepper

Pour the rice into a sieve or bowl, and wash it until the water is clear. Drain all the water out of the rice.

Pour the can of chicken broth into a 2-cup measuring cup. Add water until you get two cups of liquid.

In a 4-quart saucepan, melt the margarine over medium heat. Add the egg noodles. There should be enough to cover just the bottom of the pan. Stir the eggs noodles until they are a golden brown color.

Add the rice to the pan, and stir the rice in with the egg noodles for just one minute. Mix lightly to coat the rice with the margarine and mix with the egg noodles.

Pour the chicken broth and water over the rice and noodles in the pan. Add about ½ teaspoon salt and pepper – more or less according to your taste. Heat until boiling, stirring once or twice. Once it boils, reduce the heat to a simmer, cover the pan tightly, and let cook for about 14 minutes. (Do not lift the cover or stir.) Remove the pan of cooked rice from heat. Fluff the rice lightly with a fork; cover and let steam for 5 to 10 minutes.

Dr. Johnson with some of his second graders.

My sister and I eating Sausage Stuffing

Illustrated by Kory

Sausage Stuffing
from Kory

This recipe came from my grandfather and grandmother in Maryland. We use this recipe for Thanksgiving and Christmas dinner. It's one of me and my sister's favorite things to eat.

Ingredients:
1½ bags of stuffing mix
1 can of celery soup
1 16 ounce roll of mild or hot sausage
1 cup of onions, chopped
1 cup of celery, chopped
1 teaspoon of poultry seasoning
1 teaspoon of sage seasoning
1 cup of water
1 can of chicken broth

Cook sausage with onions and celery till done. After cooked well done in frying pan, combine all other ingredients together and bake at 350° until golden brown, about 45 minutes.

Sausage Stuffing

Illustrated by Kory

Officer Janet Rodriguez of the Hartford Police Department talks to second graders at University of Hartford Magnet School about how she and other police officers help members of the community. The students saw photos of vehicles and equipment that the police department uses to help keep our community safe.

Spanish Yellow Rice

from Officer Janet Rodriguez, Hartford Police Department

Ingredients:
1 packet of sazón
4 cups of rice
1 can of tomato sauce
2 large tablespoons of Sofrito (Spanish condiment, often found in frozen Spanish food section at your grocers)
1 tablespoon of Adobo seasoning
1 teaspoon of salt
¼ cup of vegetable oil
1 can of beans (whatever type you like, or green pigeon peas)

In a six-quart pot on high heat add oil, Sofrito, tomato sauce, sazón, salt, and Adobo. Cook for three minutes then add the can of beans. Using the can, fill with water and add to the mixture. Add three cans of water. Let this come to a simmer, lower the heat to medium high and add the rice. Mix and let dry for about 2-3 minutes (you'll see little bubbles coming through). Lower the heat to low, then mix and cover. Let the rice cook for about 20 minutes, mixing at least twice. Rice will be done when nice and fluffy.

Note: You can add vegetables, ham, or anything you might like to the mixture before adding the rice.

This rice goes great with pork chops...Enjoy your rice!

Illustrated by Joe

Sweet Potato Casserole
from Joe

My mom made up this recipe. We use it for Thanksgiving, Christmas, and parties. My mom made the recipe up for the first Thanksgiving that she and Dad were married. A few years later she began adding the cranberries. I like the marshmallows the best.

Ingredients:
¼ cup melted butter
¼ cup brown sugar
½ cup oatmeal
½ cup flour
¼ teaspoon nutmeg
¼ teaspoon cinnamon

3 medium sweet potatoes, OR 2 cups canned sweet potatoes
½ cup whole cranberries
Marshmallows

Mix the first six ingredients together to make a crumb like topping.

Prepare the three medium sweet potatoes by partially cooking them (I microwave them), then peeling and cutting them into one inch thick slices. If using canned sweet potatoes, drain the sweet potatoes and cut them into one inch thick slices.

Preheat oven to 350 degrees. In a casserole dish layer crumb mixture, sweet potatoes and cranberries. Repeat layers ending with crumb topping.

Bake for 45 minutes. Top with marshmallows and brown (5 minutes).

Ruth Rabinowitz, a member of History and Heritage through the Arts Team, picking pumpkins with some students from Mrs. Febo-Mejia's class.

Tsimmes

from Ruth Rabinowitz, History and Heritage through the Arts Team

This is a traditional side dish made for the meals served at the celebration of Jewish holidays. It has been passed down through the generations. It is a wonderful combination of sweet potatoes, carrots and dried fruits. Meat, which has been sautéed with onions, can be added to make it a heartier dish.

Ingredients:
4 yams or sweet potatoes
1 bunch carrots
½ package dried prunes
¼ package dried apricots
2 tablespoons margarine or butter
½ cup orange juice
3 tablespoons brown sugar
Salt

Boil yams and carrots until just done. Peel and slice the sweet potatoes and carrots, into ½ inch pieces. Mix in the dried fruits. Place in a 9x13 baking dish.

Mix the margarine, orange juice, and brown sugar together in a pan. Stir over a low heat until blended. Pour over the vegetables and fruit in the baking dish. Sprinkle with salt. Cover and bake for 30-45 minutes at 350 degrees, then uncover and bake another 15 minutes.

To add meat: Brown one pound of flank or brisket in a lightly oiled pan with one small chopped onion. Add boiling water to cover meat and cook for one hour. Cut into pieces and add to the above. A casserole dish may be used instead of the 9x13 oblong pan and bake as above. If mixture is very juicy, a thin paste of one tablespoon flour and a little water can be stirred in to thicken. Serves 6-8.

Desserts

Arroz con Dulce (Sweet Rice pudding, Puerto Rican style) from Mayor Eddie A. Perez, City of Hartford

Applesauce Cake from Jenny

Biscottis from Joshua

Blitz Torte from Bill Gerber, History and Heritage through the Arts Team

Chocolate Mousse Cake from John Paul Froehlich, supporter of History and Heritage through the Arts Team

Chocolate Snowflake Cookies from Emily

Fran's Famous Brownies from Barbara Pigford, History and Heritage through the Arts Team

Fruit Salsa with Cinnamon Chips from Hannah

Grammie Doe's Lollipops from Doe Hentschel, Leadership Greater Hartford

Purim Hamantaschen Cookie Dough from Jessica

Rice Pudding from Ben A.

Sweet Potato Pie from Shaquil

Sweet Potato Pie from Zoya

Mayor Perez visited the University of Hartford Magnet School to talk to second grade students about his role in the Hartford Community.

Arroz con Dulce

(Sweet Rice pudding, Puerto Rican style)
from Mayor Eddie A. Perez, City of Hartford

Ingredients:
4 cups water
1 teaspoon salt
1 teaspoon cloves
1 tablespoon crushed fresh ginger
1 14-ounce can coconut cream, such as Coco Lopez
1 cup regular, uncooked, short-grain rice
1 cup sugar
1 tablespoon cooking oil (optional)
½ cup raisins

For best results, soak rice in water for about two hours prior to cooking. Drain.

Add the salt, cloves and ginger to three cups of water in a deep saucepan. Bring to a boil. Sieve through a colander to remove the remnants of the spices, reserving the liquid.

Bring to a boil once again. Add the coconut cream, rice, sugar and oil. Cook covered over medium-low heat for about twenty minutes. Add the raisins and blend in. Continue to cook, uncovered, until the rice has absorbed all the water (about fifteen more minutes).

Cooking times vary depending on your climate and elevation from sea level. Don't worry, this recipe is very forgiving of cooking lapses. Just don't overcook!

Pour into a square or rectangular dish about one inch high and allow to cool. Sprinkle ground cinnamon or cinnamon sugar on the pudding and cut in two-inch squares for your diners.

It is equally enjoyable after refrigeration. It will keep for several days, well covered in the refrigerator.

Illustrated by Jenny

Applesauce Cake
from Jenny

My Grandma made this special cake recipe for my Mom's wedding. It's been passed down in our family from Mother to Daughter for generations.

Ingredients:
3 cups applesauce
1 cup shortening
2 cups brown sugar
2 cups raisins
4 cups flour
1 teaspoon salt
4 teaspoons baking soda
1 teaspoon ground cloves
2 teaspoons cinnamon and nutmeg
1 cup nutmeats

Combine first four ingredients and cook until well blended. Cool this mixture.

Sift together flour, salt, baking soda and cloves. Stir into wet, cooled mixture.

Add cinnamon, nutmeg, and nuts.

Pour into baking pan that has been greased and floured. Bake 50 –60 minutes at 325 degrees.

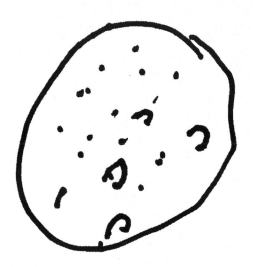

Illustrated by Josh

Biscotti's

from Josh

This recipe is from Great Grandma Piccolello, who brought it over from Italy. We usually make this recipe around all the holidays, but also just any old time you want something tasty.

Ingredients:
4 cups flour
1 tablespoon baking powder
3 eggs
1 cup vegetable oil
1 cup sugar
1 teaspoon vanilla
2 teaspoons anise
1 cup chopped almonds

Beat oil and sugar together. Add eggs one at a time while beating. Add vanilla. Gradually add flour, baking powder, anise and nuts.

Break dough into three balls and form three-inch logs. Grease cookie sheet and bake at 350 degrees for 25 minutes.

Slice logs at an angle into one inch-wide pieces. Rebake 10 minutes or until brown.

Great Aunt Caroline is the current biscotti master in our family. She taught it to Grandma Interrante, who passed it down to Mom. Mom has become a truly masterful biscotti baker.

Blitz Torte

from Bill Gerber, History and Heritage through the Arts Team

My mother, an immigrant from Europe, brought this recipe to the USA. Blitz Torte was one of the cakes that good German cooks served. "Blitz" means "Lightning" in German. This recipe could be prepared quickly on short notice. Guests in the old days didn't concern themselves with diet and cholesterol problems, and one of the marks of a good cook was her rich, tasty desserts.

Ingredients:
½ cup sugar
½ cup butter
6 eggs, separated
3 tablespoons milk
1 cup flour
1 teaspoon baking powder
¾ cup powdered sugar
1 cup slivered almonds

Custard ingredients:
1 egg
1 cup milk
½ cup sugar
1 tablespoon flour
Pinch of salt
1 teaspoon vanilla extract

Preheat oven to 350 degrees.

Cream sugar and butter, add egg yolks and milk. Mix flour and baking powder together, then add to batter. Spread in two buttered 9-inch pans.

Adding powdered sugar, gradually beat egg whites until stiff. Spread on top of batter, sprinkle almonds, and bake for 20 to 25 minutes. Cool.

Mix custard ingredients together, then boil until thick, stirring constantly. Spread on top of cooled torte.

Grandma making a cake

Illustrated by Pedro

Dr. Bill Gerber, member of History and Heritage through the Arts Team, discusses significance of community photos with a second grader.

Chocolate Mousse Cake

from John Paul Froehlich, supporter of History and Heritage through the Arts Team

This cake is adapted from a Craig Claiborne NY Times Magazine Food section printed in the mid 70's. Any one who may have attempted this recipe following the original, which required an hour and 15 minute bake time had a disaster on their hands. After my modification on the time, replacement of semisweet chocolate for the unsweetened, food processor, and microwave methods, this recipe became an instant success. I have shared this with many; in fact a version is on a Web Site.

Ingredients:
1/2 pound semisweet chocolate
1/2 pound no salt butter
scant 1/2 cup sugar
8 egg yolks
5 egg whites

Preheat oven to 350 degrees.

Put chocolate, butter, and sugar in saucepan. Set in skillet of simmering water. Stir until chocolate is melted or in Pyrex bowl and microwave on medium.

Using a food processor, whip egg yolks until light and lemon colored.

Add the hot chocolate sauce to form chocolate mousse. This will look like very thick mayonnaise.

Beat egg whites to soft peaks, stiff but not "brittle." If too stiff they will not be easy to fold into the mousse mixture. Add egg whites to chocolate, starting with a quarter of the mixture and fold until incorporated. Add a second quarter; fold then add the rest producing a light mousse.

Use two 8-inch round cake pans that have been greased and set with a circle of folded waxed paper on bottom. Use the bottom of the pan to trace diameter on the folded waxed paper, and cut two at once. Spray Pam is perfect to secure the paper on pan bottom.

Reserve 1/2 of the light chocolate mousse. This will be used as filling and frosting. Place the remaining 1/2 in the two round cake pans. Bake for 20 minutes, until toothpick comes out clean and should double in height. Upon removal, the cake will collapse.

Let stand 10 minutes, invert and cake should fall out with no coaxing. Remove the top wax paper and let cool.

Place half of the reserved mixture on top of first cake. Place second cake on top to form layer, and use the remaining mixture to finish. You may want to sift about a tablespoon of confectioner's sugar on top for a finishing touch.

Yield: 8 to 10 servings.

Good Food...

"tastes good, smells good and is sweet."
— Jazzmin, age 7

"is cheesy."
— Emily, age 7

"is food that tastes really sweet and has a good smell."
— Ben Z., age 7

"is special. It is smelly and it is wonderful."
— Zoya, age 8

"is something that doesn't make you sick."
— Rhyan, age 8

Illustrated by Emily

Chocolate Snowflake Cookies
from Emily

This recipe originally came from my mom's side of the family. These cookies are made during Christmas time. My mom makes Russian tea cakes which are white balls rolled in sugar. She also makes chocolate balls rolled in powdered sugar which in the end makes a snowflake. These are some of the cookies we have for Santa.

Ingredients:
2 cups sugar
½ cup vegetable oil
4 one-ounce squares unsweetened chocolate, melted
4 eggs
2 cups flour
2 teaspoons baking powder
½ teaspoon salt
¾ cup sifted powdered sugar
2 teaspoons vanilla extract

Combine sugar, vegetable oil and melted chocolate in a large bowl. Add eggs, then vanilla. Mix well.

Combine flour, baking powder and salt in another bowl. Add ¼ of the dry mixture at a time to chocolate mix. Cover and chill dough for at least two hours.

Shape into one-inch balls and roll in powdered sugar. Place on greased sheet. Bake at 350 degrees for 10 – 12 minutes.

Fran's Famous Brownies
from Barbara Pigford, History and Heritage through the Arts

My mother inherited a talent for making wonderful desserts, from her mother (my grandmother), who was Hungarian. This was my mother's most popular recipe. She was always asked to bring a plate of brownies whenever she was invited out. She gave out this recipe freely, but no one was able to duplicate it, so that the brownies came out as moist and tasty as hers. She was even accused by some of using a special "magic" pan, or of not giving out the correct ingredients. Here's hoping you will have better results than her friends had with this recipe.

<u>Ingredients:</u> (Note: Do not deviate from these instructions for best results.)

Melt in a large skillet (not in mixer)
½ pound butter (2 sticks)
1 square bitter chocolate

Add:
2 cups sugar
½ cup cocoa
Keep mixing in skillet

Add:
4 eggs, one at a time
1 teaspoon baking powder
1 cup flour
1 teaspoon baking powder
Note: Sift flour and baking powder together before adding.
1 teaspoon salt
1 teaspoon vanilla
1 cup nuts (walnut or pecan pieces – your choice)

Place above in 9 x 13 greased pan. Bake at 350 degrees exactly 25 minutes.

Immediately remove from oven. Cool, then place pan on shelf in refrigerator.
When cold, take out, cut in squares and serve.

Mom serving a tray of brownies

Illustrated by Alexa

Fruit Salsa with Cinnamon Chips

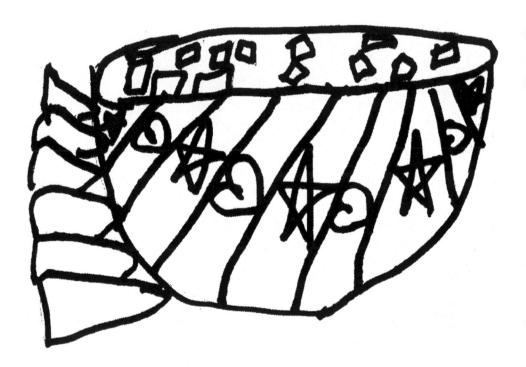

Illustrated by Hanna

Fruit Salsa with Cinnamon Chips
from Hannah

This recipe came from my Aunt Jackie. It is my favorite food and I ask for it for every special occasion we have.

Ingredients:
9 strawberries, hull & chop
2 Granny Smith apples, core & chop (do not peel)
1 kiwi, peel & chop
2 tablespoons apple jelly
2 tablespoons brown sugar
zest of 1 orange & juice of 1 orange
8" flour tortillas
butter, melted
cinnamon sugar

Fruit Salsa: Mix chopped strawberries, apples and kiwi in bowl. Stir in jelly, brown sugar, orange zest and orange juice. Cover and refrigerate until ready to serve.

Cinnamon Chips: Preheat oven to 400°. Brush a tortilla with melted butter and sprinkle with cinnamon sugar. Flip over and do the same on other side. Using a pizza cutter, cut into eight pieces. Place pieces on cookie sheet (non-stick works best). Continue buttering and sugaring more tortillas until sheet is full. Bake for 5-7 minutes. Let cool on pan, then remove to airtight container. You may want to do several sheets as these go quickly. Serve together and enjoy!

My Auntie Jack went to a cooking party and learned the recipe. She loved it so she made it for her family. I love it so much that I always ask for it for my birthday treat and for special celebrations.

Grammie Doe's Lollipops
from Doe Hentschel, Leadership Great Hartford

Many years ago when my children were young, I found a recipe for "stained glass lollipops." The magazine picture inspired me to try my hand at making these old-fashioned lollipops that looked just like stained glass. I found it easier than I'd expected and my children loved them! The lollipops quickly became a Christmas tradition and I made them every year. Now that I'm a grandmother, I've started making them again, not only for my own grandchildren, but for the youngsters in the neighborhood and the children of my co-workers. Having introduced them last year I was asked, "Are you going to make lollipops again?"

Preparation:
aluminum foil
20 lollipop sticks (can purchase the sticks at kitchen supply stores like "Kitchen etc.")

Butter a sheet of aluminum foil and lay the sticks along all four sides, ends extended off the foil and facing in toward the center. Place sticks about two inches apart.

Ingredients:
½ cup water
½ cup sugar
½ cup light corn syrup
¼ teaspoon flavoring extract
few drops of food coloring

In a small saucepan, combine water, sugar and corn syrup. Place over medium heat and stir until sugar is dissolved. Do not stir anymore. Boil until the mixture reaches the "hard crack" stage. The amount is too small to use a candy thermometer, so to know when the hard crack stage is reached, dip a tablespoon into the boiling mixture and scoop out a little bit. Pour it into a cup of cold water, it should immediately form a thin hard string of candy that will crack. (If it has not cooked long enough, the mixture will be gummy or will be hard, but will not crack. Wait a little longer and test again. Once it reaches hard crack, remove it from the heat immediately as the mixture might caramelize and turn golden brown.)

When done, remove from the heat and stir in ¼ teaspoon of your choice of flavoring extract and a few drops of corresponding food color (for example green color goes with mint flavoring, red with strawberry, yellow with banana, etc.) Scoop about one tablespoon of the mixture onto the top of each stick on the foil, forming a lollipop, with the stick extending into the lollipop. They will harden quickly. Let stand for 30 minutes and they will then lift easily from the foil. Wrap each in plastic wrap and tie a bow around the stick for a special treat.

Variations:
--Make a second (and third, fourth, etc.) batch using a different color and flavor. Spoon it around the first lollipop like a rainbow to make a larger "all day" lollipop.
--While the lollipop is not quite set, sprinkle cookie decorations on the candy.

Note: If the cooked mixture hardens in the pan before you have completed spooning it onto the foil, simply return the pan to the heat for a few seconds until it is once again soft enough to spoon out. When finished, run hot water into pan to dissolve the residue.

Illustrated by Anjelica

Purim Hamantaschen Cookie Dough
from Jessica

My mom makes these cookies on the Purim holiday. We go to synagogue dressed up and hear the story of King Ahasuerus and Queen Esther read. Whenever we hear the name Haman (the bad guy) said in the story, we make lots of noise, especially with our noisemakers called graggers. These cookies are really good. We usually have them in a celebration after we get home from the synagogue.

Ingredients:
½ cup margarine, softened
½ cup sugar
1 egg
1 egg yolk
½ coup sour cream
1 tsp. vanilla
2 ½ cups flour
½ tsp. baking soda
2 tsp. baking powder
Pinch of salt
¾ tsp. nutmeg or mace

Cream margarine and sugar. Add egg and yolk and blend well. Combine sour cream and vanilla and add the margarine mixture alternately with all dry ingredients mixed together. Wrap in waxed paper and refrigerate at least 2 hours. Divide dough into 3 parts and roll out 1 part at a time. Cut in large rounds, using rim of glass. We use a glass with approximately a three-inch diameter. Place some filling (listed next) in center of each round. Brush top with slightly beaten egg white diluted with 1 tsp. water. Place on greased cookie sheet and bake at 350 degrees for 15 minutes or until golden.

Filling:

1. chocolate chips (Jessica's favorite)
2. nuts
3. Jam-- raspberry, strawberry, or peach
4. Pie filling-- poppyseed, prune, etc.
5. Mix poppyseed filling with raspberry jam, and add nuts. Put approximately one teaspoon per cookie. (Jessica's mother's favorite).

Illustrated by Alexa

Illustrated by Ben A.

Rice Pudding
from Ben A.

This recipe originally came from my mom's family. Our family makes this rice pudding mostly at Christmas time. Everyone loves it and asks for it.

Ingredients:
1 cup uncooked white rice
½ gallon whole milk
pinch of salt
1 cup sugar
1 teaspoon vanilla
six eggs

Combine all ingredients except eggs in a large saucepot. Cook over low heat until rice is tender (approximately 3 hours). If necessary, loosen with milk. Add beaten eggs while mixture is still hot. Stir well. Cool overnight. Serve with cinnamon and whipped cream. Serves a crowd.

Illustrated by Shaquil

Sweet Potato Pie
from Shaquil

This recipe originally came from my great grandmother. My family usually makes this recipe on holidays and for bake sales.

Ingredients:
1 frozen pie shell
2 medium sweet potatoes, cooked until tender and peeled
1 egg
1 cup sugar
1 stick butter or margarine
1 ½ tablespoons vanilla flavoring
1 teaspoon lemon flavoring
2 teaspoons cinnamon
2 teaspoons all spice
1 teaspoon nutmeg
½ teaspoon ginger

Preheat oven to 400 degrees. Combine all above ingredients, except pie shell, and mix well until thick and creamy. Pour into frozen pie shell. Bake pie in oven for 35 minutes. Let cool until firm.

Illustrated by Zoya

Sweet Potato Pie

from Zoya

This recipe is from my grandmother. My family eats sweet potato pie on Thanksgiving and Christmas, when we get together for those two holidays. Yes, my grandmother picks the potatoes out of the garden right before Thanksgiving and she prepares the pies for the holidays. She makes extra pies to freeze until the night before Christmas. Then she takes them out for Christmas day.

Ingredients:
1 nine inch, deep-dish unbaked piecrust
2 to 3 medium sized sweet potatoes
1 stick butter (room temperature)
2 eggs
¾ cup Carnation milk
1¼ cups of sugar
1 tablespoon of nutmeg

Boil sweet potatoes until soft. Let potatoes cool enough to handle them. Peel potatoes and place in mixing bowl.

Add butter, eggs, Carnation milk, sugar and nutmeg. Beat until texture is creamy. If texture is thick, add more Carnation milk and continue to beat until creamy.

Pour in unbaked pie shell and bake at 350 degrees for one hour. Let cool and serve.

Beverages

Egg Nog from Ted Carroll, Director, Leadership Greater Hartford

Iced Tea Recipe from Robert Wilder, History and Heritage through the Arts Team

Jammin' Jamaican Ginger Beer from Nasri

Milkshakes from Ben Z.

Old Fashion Ice Cream Soda from Ethel M. Austin, History and Heritage through the Arts Team

Illustrated by Ty'rek

Ted's Egg Nog
from Ted Carroll, Director, Leadership Greater Hartford

Ingredients:
6 eggs
½ pound confectioners sugar
1 tablespoon vanilla
1 quart whipping cream
grated nutmeg

Separate the yolks from whites of eggs. Beat the egg yolks, gradually adding the confectioner's sugar. Add the vanilla. Next add the whipping cream, beating constantly.

Beat separately the six egg whites. Fold them into the other ingredients. Sprinkle with grated nutmeg.

Serve chilled, and refrigerate leftovers for next day's enjoyment.

Good Food is...

"food that has good taste, and nice smell."
— Taylia, age 7

"food that has seeds like apples, because you can plant the seeds and grow an apple tree." — Isaiah, age 7

"food that makes you healthy and strong. Good food smells really sweet like a lollipop — Nasri, age 6

"something that attracts your taste and tastes very good."
— Ethan, age 8

Iced Tea Recipe

from Robert Wilder, History and Heritage through the Arts Team

1 bag lemon tea
1 bag raspberry tea
1 bag cinnamon tea
4 bags any regular tea (Lipton, Salada)

Put all of the above bags in about four cups of boiling water and let them steep for a while. Take off burner and when it cools down add:

1 tub of lemon Crystal Light

Mix together and put all in 2½ quart container, adding additional water until the container is full.

Refrigerate and enjoy!

Illustrated by Nasri

Jammin' Jamaican Ginger Beer
from Nasri

Ingredients:
2 medium size fresh Ginger Root
½ cup lime juice
2 ½ cups sugar
1 quart of water

Extract the juice from ginger root. Combine the water with ginger juice. Add the limejuice to the mixture. Sweeten with the sugar. Refrigerate until chilled.
Note: Ginger is spicy. Use ginger juice according to your taste preference.

Second graders perform a jammin' dance routine.

Illustrated by Ben Z

Milk Shakes
from Benjamin Z.

These recipes are from my new junior cookbook. I made them when my grandma and grandpa were here for Thanksgiving. Milk shakes are good to drink when you are hot and are easy for kids to make by themselves. This is the first recipe I made by myself.

Equipment needed:
Measuring cups
Electric Blender
Ice cream scoop or large spoon
Rubber scraper
2 tall glasses

Ingredients:
¾ cup milk
2 cups vanilla or chocolate ice cream

Pour milk into the blender container. Add half of the ice cream. Cover with the lid. Blend till smooth. Stop and scrape the sides using the rubber scraper, as needed.

Add the rest of the ice cream. Cover and blend just till smooth, stopping and scraping as needed. Pour into glasses. Makes 2 servings.

More Milk Shake Flavors to make:

Banana Shakes: Make the shakes as directed above, except add half a banana each time you add ice cream. (use one whole banana).

Peanut Butter Shakes: Make the shakes as directed above, except add 2 tablespoons peanut butter to the milk.

Malted Milk Shakes: Make the shakes as directed above, except add 2 tablespoons instant malted milk powder to the milk.

Illustrated by Destinee

Good food is...

"sugar and sweetness."

— Joe, age 7

"ice cream, because it is cold and in different flavors."

— Zach, age 8

"pizza, because you can put all kinds of stuff on it."

— Zhanel, age 7

Old-Fashion Ice Cream Soda
from Ethel M. Austin

As a single senior, I have had little experience in knowing what young people like to eat. I was fortunate to get a high school junior to do some paper work for me, from a school just down the street. The first time she came, as it was early afternoon, I offered what I had: chocolate pudding with whipped cream, jello with or without whipped cream, or an old-fashion ice cream soda. She said she had never had one of the sodas, so now we have one whenever she comes. We both love it! So will your kids…and you! Here is how I make it.

Ingredients:
Friendly's Butter Crunch ice cream
1 small can chilled Coca Cola
2 tablespoons heavy cream

Use a large glass or cup that can hold at least 12 ounces. Fill one third of the glass or cup with Friendly's Butter Crunch ice cream (about two large scoops), but do not pack it down.

Add two tablespoons of heavy cream.

Open a small can of chilled Coca Cola. Pour into the glass or cup, allowing it to form a fizz on the top. Serve immediately with a straw and long ice-tea spoon.

Index

Printed in the United States
47117LVS00002B/235-609